Growing
Beans

Focus: Designing, Making and Appraising

PETER SLOAN &
SHERYL SLOAN

I had ten bean
seeds. I planted
the seeds.

I had ten eggshells.
I filled each shell
with soil.

I used the end of
a pencil to make a
hole in the soil in
each eggshell.

I planted one seed
in each hole.
I covered each seed
with soil.

I put water on
each seed. I used
two teaspoons for
each seed.

I put the eggshells
in a box. I put
the box in the sun,
near a window.

I put water on the
seeds every day. In
a few days I saw a
small bean plant.